MW00773045

MEDITATIVE MAZES
AND
LABYRINTHS

MEDITATIVE MAZES
AND
LABYRINTHS

Cassandra Camille Wass

STERLING INNOVATION
An imprint of Sterling Publishing Co., Inc.

New York / London
www.sterlingpublishing.com

STERLING, the Sterling logo, STERLING INNOVATION, and the Sterling Innovation logo are registered trademarks of Sterling Publishing Co., Inc.

10 9 8 7 6 5 4 3 2 1

Published by Sterling Publishing Co., Inc.
387 Park Avenue South, New York, NY 10016
© 2009 by Sterling Publishing Co., Inc.

Packaged by LightSpeed Publishing, Inc.
Designed by X-Height Studio

Distributed in Canada by Sterling Publishing
c/o Canadian Manda Group, 165 Dufferin Street
Toronto, Ontario, Canada M6K 3H6
Distributed in the United Kingdom by GMC Distribution Services
Castle Place, 166 High Street, Lewes, East Sussex, England BN7 1XU
Distributed in Australia by Capricorn Link (Australia) Pty. Ltd.
P.O. Box 704, Windsor, NSW 2756, Australia

Printed in China
All rights reserved

Sterling ISBN 978-1-4027-6529-2

For information about custom editions, special sales, premium and corporate purchases, please contact Sterling Special Sales Department at 800-805-5489 or specialsales@sterlingpublishing.com.

CONTENTS

INTRODUCTION 1

ANCIENT MAZES AND LABYRINTHS
ACROSS CULTURES 4
Labyrinths in Greece 6
Labyrinths in the Roman Empire 8
Church Labyrinths 9
Outdoor Mazes and Labyrinths 11
Labyrinths in Other Cultures 13

THE LEGENDARY LABYRINTH 16
Sacred Labyrinth Geometry 18
Sacred Circle Designs 19
Classical or Cretan Designs 19
Concentric Designs 20

Roman Designs 20

Prayer Designs 21

Man-in-the-Maze Design 22

THE METHODICAL MAZE 23

Traditional Maze Terms 24

Maze Terms 25

Types of Mazes 26

Simply-Connected Maze 26

Multiply-Connected Maze or Braid Maze 26

Turf Mazes and Mizmazes 27

Weave Maze 27

Planar Maze 28

CREATING A JOURNEY ON THE PATH 29

Meditation 29

Meditative Maze and Labyrinth Guide 30

Part I. Getting Started 30

Part II. The Meditative Process 31

Part III. Meditative Drawing 31

THE POWER OF COLOR AND DESIGN 33

The Power of Design 34

Color Power 34

MAZE AND LABYRINTH MEDITATIONS

MAZE AND LABYRINTH MEDITATIONS 36

Working with Labyrinths 37

Working with Mazes 37

Healing Meditations 38

Spiritual Intuitive Meditations 40

Meditations for Transformation 42

Modern Meditations 43

Labyrinth Designs 43

Maze Designs 49

Illustration Credits 56

INTRODUCTION

If you ask most people to define a maze, they would answer by saying it is some sort of puzzle or game. But ask about a labyrinth and you are likely to get quizzical looks. Mazes are commonplace today—we see them in puzzle books, as games (including computer-generated games), and even in cornfields (Figures 1 and 2).

Labyrinths, on the other hand, have had a much more low-key existence, being used mainly in spiritual practices in the past. They are making a comeback, however. Outdoor labyrinths have been constructed in cites around the world. Some are used for pleasure and others as memorials. Newer churches also have graced their floors with temporary and permanent labyrinths for pilgrimages.

Mazes and labyrinths are ancient symbols that were once used as tools to gain deeper understanding of human spirituality. History shows that people used them to balance, heal, empower, and create transformation for themselves. One very important quality is that they help to calm the mind and center the body. In the busy world of the 21st century, we are often pulled in many different directions and need something to bring us back to our center and to restore harmony. The maze and the labyrinth were designed just for this purpose, and meditating with these unique patterns is gaining popularity again.

FIGURE 1. *A yin-yang puzzle maze*

FIGURE 2. *Child in a corn maze*

At first glance, labyrinths and mazes seem to be very similar, if not the same thing. But there are significant differences. The word "labyrinth" comes from the Greek word "labrys," which means "a double ax." "Labyrinth" comes from the story of the Minotaur from the palace of King Minos, which was referred to as the "House of the Double Ax." Ancient labyrinths date to the Neolithic period, about 2500 BCE, and have distinct qualities. The maze evolved from the labyrinth a bit later—it can be found in the Byzantine period, around 1200 CE. Both contain many similarities but also structural differences.

If you compare a maze to a labyrinth, you will notice they have basic design patterns in common. For instance, both are constructed with lines making intricate pathways that lead somewhere. The winding paths are contained in some sort of shape or outer wall, usually circular or angular, and there are at least one entrance and one exit, sometimes at the same place.

Labyrinths can be considered to be the simpler of the two patterns, while mazes contain different variations that were later added onto the labyrinth. For example, the mere labyrinth has one path leading to a center and then out again. Mazes, more complex in their nature, have added pathways, dead ends, cul-de-sacs, and sometimes a variety of entrances and exits. It has been said that the labyrinth is used to find one's way, while the maze is for escape and getting lost.

The design differences of the two also create separate meditative uses. Generally, labyrinths with one winding path are used for creating journeys, themes of birth, healing, and traveling with the natural flow of life. Mazes, on the other hand, provide numerous alternatives to follow on the path, lending themselves to goals, choices, and solutions. As you will see, both are great exercises in meditative practice for the mind and spirit.

This book explores the ancient labyrinth and maze and their sacred designs. You'll also learn how to create a spiritual journey using these ancient representations. You'll find various tools and instructions for using the drawings in this kit. Finally, there are powerful meditations to follow when coloring the drawings.

ANCIENT MAZES AND LABYRINTHS ACROSS CULTURES

Throughout the timeline of history, mazes and labyrinths have been found in many cultures across the world. Archaeologists have discovered examples of these symbols in the Mediterranean, the Middle East, Europe, parts of Asia, and the Americas. The first evidence of these patterns dates back to 2500 BCE at the end of the Neolithic period and the beginning of Bronze Age, when we see the first permanent human settlements. There is no clear evidence as to why these patterns came about, but some speculate that these were ancient symbols of early goddess societies that represented life and birth. In the Iron Age of the Greeks and following all the way to the Renaissance period in Europe, these symbols began to have much more meaning and were used in everyday life.

Archaeological findings show that societies across the world used these ancient symbols in many different ways. Commonly, cultures would organize walking labyrinths and mazes, creating them on the ground for meditative practices and spiritual pilgrimages. Some were made of paved stone; others were carved into the earth. Homes, churches, and palaces were tiled with exquisite floor designs and some were grown as beautiful gardens. These were used for ceremonies of celebration such as marriages, and they were danced on during rites of passage. Painted labyrinths decorated the outsides of homes and temples. These were thought to keep away evil. Many believed that negative spirits moved in a linear fashion—by placing a labyrinth or maze on a building, spirits would be trapped and prevented from getting in. Drawings on pottery and walls recorded birth scenes, and engraved Greek coins paid homage to ancient myths.

The origins of labyrinths and mazes remain a mystery. The earliest existences of labyrinths have been found on prehistoric rock outcrop carvings in Pontevedra and Vigo, Spain. The ancient designs are that of the seven-circuit labyrinth. Archaeologists have found these hard to date but believe that they are over 4500 years old. Because there is no language explaining the patterns, it is unknown why the inhabitants carved them and when they came into being. Some believe the design is that of a womb honoring a birth and its passage to life while others believe it is some sort of map showing the road to the underworld for the deceased. One thing we do know is that the early labyrinths of this BCE period all have the same "classical" seven-circuit design; it was certainly a symbol of importance (Figure 3).

One of the oldest known labyrinths is from Luzzanas, Sardinia, and may date back to 2000 BCE. Carved on a rock wall in an underground Neolithic tomb, nicknamed the "Tomba del Labirinto" (Tomb of the Labyrinth), this labyrinth was one of those thought to be a passage map leading to the underworld. It is believed that this carving may not be from the Neolithic period but may be graffiti that was carved at a later date. Another early labyrinth was found in Tell Rifa'at, Syria, on a shard from a ceramic vessel. This piece is believed to be from about 1200 BCE. One of the most famous ancient labyrinths was found

FIGURE 3. *Seven-ring classical labyrinth found in Rocky Valley, Cornwall, UK, age unknown*

on the Hollywood Stone in a field in County Wicklow, Ireland. This stone is believed to date back to 2000 BCE and may have been used as a road marker for the early Christians.

The most accurate origin date found is for a labyrinth from Greece. Archaeologists have been able to successfully date an engraved clay tablet from the Mycenaean palace of Pylos to 1200 BCE. On one side of the tablet is a labyrinth in the shape of a square, and on the other side is a record of delivery for goats. This suggests that the labyrinth may have been a symbol for a business or perhaps used as a game or puzzle.

LABYRINTHS IN GREECE

An explosion of mazes and labyrinths found its way into Greece during the Iron Age and Hellenistic period. In Knossos, Crete, coins dating back to 300 BCE were inscribed with labyrinths on one side and gods on the other. One of the earliest maze drawings appears next to a poem on a Greek manuscript from the 11th century. Many artifact fragments and frescoes at the Minoan Palace, which was destroyed by a fire, show labyrinth and maze patterns such as on the Mycenaean tablet. A labyrinth honoring the Trojan War even found its way to Italy on a 7th century Etruscan jar marked with the word *Truis*, or Troy. These symbols were integrated and used in Greek daily culture.

In Greek mythology, the Trojans (great rivals of the Greeks) asked the gods Poseidon and Apollo for help building a great wall around their city for protection. They carved a dense wall out of the rock and earth into the shape of a maze. Upon completion, Poseidon asked the city for compensation. The Trojans, thinking the wall was impenetrable, refused his request. This enraged the god, and he sent a sea monster to attack the city. "Troy Town" or "Turf Mazes," which are raised out of the grass or ground, honor the Troy story. These became popular throughout Europe during the Crusades and later in the 18th and 19th centuries.

Perhaps one of the most profound myths surrounding the labyrinth is that of the Minotaur. According to legend, a labyrinth was built at the palace of Knossos in Crete to imprison the half-man, half-bull beast known as the Minotaur (Figure 4). A sacrifice of seven men and women from Athens was made every nine years to the beast in retribution for the death of Androgeus, the son of King Minos. The frightened volunteers would be paraded around the town of Knossos and then sent into the labyrinth. When they reached the center, these terrified souls would be devoured whole by the Minotaur. Theseus, son of King Aegeus of Athens, was a strong young man of courage. He volunteered to go into the labyrinth with the intention of slaying the Minotaur. He knew that if he succeeded, it would end an era of dominant Minoan power and worship.

When Theseus arrived in Crete, he fell in love with Ariadne, daughter of King Minos. She promised to help him if he took her away from the island. Theseus was not familiar with the dark labyrinth and was afraid he would not be able to make his way out. Ariadne, keeping her promise, gave Theseus a ball of golden thread to unravel on the path. He made his way to the center of the labyrinth where he encountered the ferocious Minotaur and, after a heated battle, succeeded in killing the beast. Theseus then followed Ariadne's thread and made his way out. The two escaped from Crete and celebrated their victory on the island of Naxos by dancing the Crane or *Geranos* dance (based on the mating dance of the crane). This dance has become a popular pastime at labyrinth ceremonial celebrations and is still danced today.

Figure 4. Bronze statue of the classic Minotaur

This Minotaur myth was so powerful that it traveled across European culture and was seen as a great story of spiritual awakening. The symbolism of following the labyrinth's path to the center meant facing one's deepest fears. To confront and assassinate those fears (the Minotaur) and find your way out, was thought to be ultimate victory and transformation of the spirit.

Labyrinths in the Roman Empire

By the time the Roman Empire rose in 63 BCE, the classical seven-circuit labyrinth had begun its transformation into what is now called the *Roman labyrinth* (Figure 5). Known for their artistic skills, the Romans elaborated on the design by creating a four-quadrant symbol. Typically this design was in the shape of a square or rectangle with all quarters meeting at the center.

Throughout the Roman Empire, from western Europe to Africa, this new design was commonly used in mosaic tiled floors. There are over sixty examples still in existence today. Many designs pay homage to the Myth of the Minotaur. The Torrazzo Tower in Cremona, Italy, houses a classic Roman mosaic labyrinth. In the center is a picture of Theseus and the Minotaur in heated battle. Two other famous examples are found in Rhaetia, Switzerland, and Conimbriga, Portugal, one of the empire's largest settlements.

The Minotaur myth also showed up in other areas of Roman culture. Men's clothing, especially bullfighting outfits, often hailed the labyrinth design. Carved on an ancient Roman gem is the symbol with a depiction of the Minotaur as half man (upper body) and half beast (lower body). An inscription on a house in Pompeii, Italy, which was buried in ash by the eruption of Mt. Vesuvius in 79 CE, still reads "Labyrinthus hic habitat Minotaurus," meaning "the labyrinth, here lives the Minotaur."

FIGURE 5. *Roman labyrinth*

Church Labyrinths

In the 4th century CE, the Roman emperor Constantine allowed Christianity to become a legal religion in Rome. Each year Christians would take a vow to make a pilgrimage to Jerusalem to honor Jesus Christ. These journeys were very popular at the time; however, as money and means became scarce, many people were unable to make the trip. In place of this long, almost impossible journey, Christians decided to use labyrinths. They constructed them in churches and outdoor spaces (known as "turf mazes") as a substitute. It was thought that to walk the path with full devotion would bring one closer to God and offer spiritual salvation. Walking the labyrinth was done in prayer and meditation and became a sacred symbol of the holy pilgrimage.

One of the first Christian labyrinths can be found in the Basilica of St. Reparatus in North Africa, approximately one hundred miles west of Algiers. It was part of the Roman Empire; the floor mosaic dates back to the 4th century, and at the center it reads "Sancta Ecclesia" or "Holy Church."

In Europe, the first prayer labyrinth lies in the Church of St. Vitale in Ravenna, Italy. Built in the 6th century, this small seven-circuit labyrinth is part of a larger paved floor design. Many churches also had small labyrinth designs known as *finger labyrinths* outside of the buildings; these could be traced with one's fingers. There were eighty Gothic cathedrals constructed throughout Europe during the Middle Ages. The labyrinth graced twenty-two of them. These designs were not only used to honor the divine holy pilgrimage, but for births, wedding unions, celebrations, and repentance where one would walk the path on their knees.

During the Medieval period, these symbols became known as *prayer labyrinths* and were the central focus in the church. This was primarily due to the fact that the Crusades had begun, and making pilgrimages to the Holy Land was not only costly but extremely dangerous. The prayer labyrinth was also a big draw as a way to connect with God, and it brought new members into the church. The classical seven-circuit design was extended, making a round eleven-circuit labyrinth that contained four quadrants modeled after the Roman labyrinth. Many were placed near the fronts of churches by the baptismal water fountains. These elaborate prayer designs represented the beginning of a path to a spiritual journey.

One of the most famous examples of the prayer labyrinth lies in the Cathedral of Our Lady of Chartres, located near Paris, France (Figure 6). Built around 1200 CE, it is paved in stone with four quadrants meant to symbolize the cross. This pattern is so famous it is copied in texts, made into outdoor turf labyrinths, and seen in churches around the world today (Figure 7).

The Chartres design and other various church labyrinths like it were called the "chemin de Jerusalem," or Road of Jerusalem. Walking the labyrinth as a pilgrimage is still common today. People from all over the world travel to France and walk this popular eleven-circuit design with the rosette flower at the middle. Cathedral designs throughout Europe such as those in Reims, Amiens, St. Omar, Canterbury, Santiago de Compostela, and St. Remy still exist and are also allowed to be walked.

By the 17th and 18th centuries, church labyrinths began to lose popularity. Once sacred, the labyrinth was now thought of as a pagan symbol. The clergy sought to eliminate what it considered a non-Christian symbol even though that symbol had brought in hundreds of new church members. Many were removed completely, deemed part of magical practices and torn from the floors. Others were covered by chairs or pews and were forgotten as pilgrimage sites. Labyrinths transformed once again, but this time into mazes.

FIGURE 6. *Chartres Cathedral*

FIGURE 7. *Chartres design in a church, San Francisco, California*

MEDITATIVE MAZES AND LABYRINTHS

Outdoor Mazes and Labyrinths

Outdoor labyrinths increased in popularity throughout Europe during the Middle Ages. Many were constructed near churches, on hillsides, or in the centers of towns. There were many names for these labyrinths, ironically called mazes, which contained a single path. The *turf mazes*, *Troy Towns*, and *mizmazes* were constructed by carving a grooved path into the earth, grass, or turf; many included rocks around them (Figures 8 and 9). Some could be as small as six inches high, while other paths measured up to five feet tall. These early mazes took on the Cretan seven-circuit design, but upon the insistence of the Church, later ones were modeled after Roman labyrinths, like the Chartres Cathedral pattern.

In the late Medieval period, using turf mazes as a model, huge gardens were constructed for the aristocratic elite. These would later be transformed into *hedge gardens* that would possess maze construction. They were designed and planted for

FIGURE 8.
Ancient Troy Town maze with rocks, St. Agnes, Isles of Scilly

FIGURE 9. *Carved Troy Town maze*

the nobility in Italy and France. A good example is found today in Versailles, France, at the palace of King Louis XIV where there are four quadrants of turf mazes surrounded by shrubs and trees in the palace gardens (Figure 10).

Hedge mazes became very popular during the 16th and 17th centuries. They could be found in Italy, France, and especially in England where they were a favorite. Many books were written about how to lay out these mazes and which plants would be best for gardening. They were grown with twisting paths, bridges, arbors, and elaborate fountains. Some of these mazes were huge estate gardens sitting on as many as twenty acres (Figure 11). At Longleat House in Wiltshire there are thousands of English Yew trees and a path spanning over 1.6 miles long.

It was common to see these mazes at the estates of nobles, and many were built for special commemorations. The traditional turf Hilton Maze was constructed in 1660 by William Sparrow to celebrate the restoration of the throne to Charles II. Anne Boleyn, Henry VIII's second wife, played in a 13th century maze at Hever Castle in Kent. One of the oldest and most famous hedge mazes lies at Hampton Court Palace in West London near the Thames. This Tudor trapezoid-shaped garden was built in honor of the arrival of William III in 1690—it is believed to be an upgraded maze from one originally built by Henry III, since this had been a royal palace for years. The last known royal to live there was George II. In the 1800s, the royal family opened the garden to the public; it continues to attract thousands of visitors every year.

FIGURE 10. *Palace at Versailles*

FIGURE 11. *An elaborate garden maze*   FIGURE 12. *Hedge maze in autumn*

The elite enjoyed these mazes as fun outdoor amusement sites for their royal guests. Gardens served as favorite places for social gatherings and for leisurely walks (Figure 12). With secret corridors and hedged paths reaching over six feet tall, these gardens also had a reputation as meeting places for flirting lovers. They were certainly a place to get lost. It is rumored that Henry II built a hedge maze garden at Woodstock to hide his mistress, Rosamund, from his possessive wife, Eleanor of Aquitaine.

LABYRINTHS IN OTHER CULTURES

The labyrinth has appeared in many ancient cultures, from North America to Asia. In India, the classical seven-circuit design can be seen on an ancient petroglyph in Goa, dating to the Neolithic period, and on a dolmen shrine in the Nilgiri Mountains from the Bronze Age. It is thought that many of these labyrinths may have been city maps. Some believe these designs, like the *kolam labyrinth*, would ward off evil spirits (Figure 13). This design appeared in various manuscripts, was worn as jewelry, and was used in homes as protection.

In southeastern India, the kolam pattern graces many doorsteps today, where an offering to the goddess Lakshmi will bring protection and good fortune for those who live in the house.

The *chakra-vyuha labyrinth* is a famous Indian battle formation mentioned in the Mahabharata, a Hindu epic (Figure 14). In this story, a seven-circuit spiral in the shape of a wheel was created by Drona and believed to be impenetrable by man and the gods. Four Pandava warriors, Abhimanyu, Arjuna, Krishna, and Pradyumna, stepped up to battle through the vyuha's (formations) layers. Unfortunately, Abhimanyu, son of Arjuna, who learned from his father how to enter the labyrinth, did not know how to exit. As Abhimanyu penetrated the sixth layer, he and the other warriors were killed. This battle scene and the chakra-vyuha labyrinth appear in many texts and artist depictions after the 17th century.

In the 5th century BCE, Herodotus wrote about a great labyrinth he saw in Egypt. In Book II of Histories, he describes a complex building surrounded by a single wall and filled with over three-thousand chambers and passageways. The great maze was situated near Lake Moeris and the ancient city of Crocodilopolis. It is believed that this was either a funeral temple built by Amenemhet III to keep out tomb robbers and evil spirits or a meeting place for Egyptians that later turned into a temple to honor the pharaoh. The stone labyrinth was eventually destroyed and used as a quarry during the Roman Era.

On the other side of the world, many labyrinth artifacts have been discovered in the Americas. On the plains of Nazca, Peru, huge carved geoglyphs of various figures include spiral labyrinth-like designs. The pictures are only visible from the sky. Some speculate these were animal totems used as symbols of prayer and rebirth in ceremonies. One carving shows a classic five-circuit symbol

FIGURE 13. *Kolam labyrinth*

FIGURE 14. *Chakra-vyuha labyrinth*

with a double-lined path leading out. The spiral tail of the well-known monkey is another example from the many figures.

A unique labyrinth was created by the Tohono O'odham and Pima tribes in Arizona in the United States around the same time as the Hellenistic period of the Greeks. The *Man in the Maze* or *Siuku Ki* shows a labyrinth with a small man standing at the top of the entrance and is usually woven into baskets. The man symbolizes the myth of Iitoi, who was the ancestral father of the tribes. According to legend, his spirit lived on the top of Baboquivari, a sacred mountain. He would take human form to enter the local village and cause trouble. Upon being charged, he would escape by running back through the labyrinth to the mountain, losing his chasers on the path. This symbolism is similar to the Minotaur in that the Native Americans believed that traveling to the center would confront your bad self or troubles (Iitoi), and making it out of the labyrinth would lead to a sacred journey (Baboquivari Mountain).

The Hopi American Indians, also located in Arizona, left behind carved rock labyrinths dating back to the 12th century (Figure 15). Two distinct designs emerged from this culture. The first, known as *mother and child* or *Ta'pu*, has seven circuits enclosed in a circular pattern. The second, called the *sun father* or *giver of life*, is a seven-circuit labyrinth contained within a square shape. These symbols emerge as representations of the male and female energies and as a celebration of birth.

FIGURE 15. *Hopi petroglyph*

THE LEGENDARY LABYRINTH

The labyrinth, simple in its design, has had many transformations throughout time. From the prehistoric rock carvings, to fearless legends, to pilgrimages of salvation in churches and meditative journeys, the labyrinth has demonstrated itself as a legendary and, certainly, powerful symbol of humanity.

Early artists created labyrinths based on spirals found in nature, and spiral labyrinths are still popular (Figure 16). If we look at the seashell or spiraled spiderweb, we can see labyrinth designs were modeled after these fundamental patterns (Figures 17 and 18). Like a winding umbilical cord connected to the unborn child, the ancient labyrinth was primal in nature and connected itself to all aspects of birth (Figure 19). Many believe this to be the original symbol of the goddess society of the Neolithic period. The round shape symbolized the female womb and was etched in rocks and caves as a symbol of protection for the mother. Each pathway represented stages of pregnancy and the journey in finding the way to new life and beginnings.

The labyrinth also had another side known as rebirth. Legends like that of the Minotaur and Mahabharata epic dealt with themes of risk, peril, threat, and battle with the hero finding his journey to spiritual redemption and salvation. Entering the labyrinth was seen as a courageous act of stepping into the unknown to face one's fears. Meeting at the center was a confrontation of those demons. To slay the dragon or beast was a representation of transforming the self. To follow the winding path out of the twisted maze would bring enlightenment and a renewed life.

The first labyrinths were actually very simply constructed for such legendary symbols. Contained in circular womb-like shapes called walls, labyrinths had a unicursal path or circuit. Flowing back and forth like a meandering pattern, the design would lead to a center or goal and then out again. The mouth served as both entrance and exit. Early labyrinths were designed with three, five, and seven- circuit paths from what is known as the "seed" pattern (Figure 20). The seed pattern was a cross with four dots that were then connected to make a labyrinth.

By the Middle Ages, as humans and art became more complex, so did labyrinths. Many were drawn with eleven circuits, four quadrants, and contained in circle or square shapes (Figure 21). These elaborate designs still kept

FIGURE 16.
Triple spiral labyrinth

FIGURE 17.
Seashell spiral

FIGURE 18.
Spiderweb spiral

FIGURE 19.
Baby in the womb

FIGURE 20.
Seed pattern

FIGURE 21.
*Famous four-quadrant
Chartres design*

their basic labyrinth structure with one meandering pathway leading to the center and traveling out again. Eventually, these ornate designs would transform into mazes with new rules and structures.

SACRED LABYRINTH GEOMETRY

Many believe labyrinths to be energy centers containing sacred geometrical patterns. Throughout time, temples, churches, and sacred areas have been built using the principles of sacred geometry.

What is sacred geometry? Basically it is the utilization of forms (e.g. the spiral pattern) from nature that are put into geometric models (e.g. the labyrinth) for the purpose of resonating spiritual energies. The desired goal of these energies is to bring enlightenment and healing to the receiver.

If you are working with a labyrinth (such as walking, drawing, or tracing it with a finger), you will experience meditative qualities through the art of sacred geometry. Some research suggests that the geometric shape produces an energy field that can heal ailments of the body and calm the mind. It balances thoughts with presence of the body to the point where one stops thinking and the intuition of knowingness takes over. Many have reported expanded aura fields and a sense of peace, and even bliss, while working with labyrinths.

Sacred Circle Designs

Humans have produced hundreds of labyrinth designs. Most of them are based on the labyrinths found from 2500 BCE to the 17th century CE. Some go beyond the circular shape with squares, polygons, and half circles. It is important to understand these designs because they have been created with different meditative purposes in mind.

Classical or Cretan Designs

These are seen from early ancient labyrinths through the Hellenistic period, created from the crossed seed pattern.

> Three-circuit classical (Figure 22)
> Five-circuit reconciliation (Figure 23)
> Seven-circuit classical (Figure 24)

Meditative Uses:
❖ Birthing new beginnings. ❖ Finding one's way in the world.
❖ Regenerating the self and rebirth.

FIGURE 22.
Three-circuit classical

FIGURE 23.
Five-circuit reconciliation

FIGURE 24.
Seven-circuit classical

Concentric Designs

These are seen from early ancient labyrinths through the Hellenistic period. They have a circular path with no cross in the center.

> Seven-circuit Baltic wheel or goddess (Figure 25)
> Seven-circuit round "concentric" classical (Figure 26)

Meditative Uses:

❖ Birthing new beginnings. ❖ Finding one's way in the world.
❖ Journeys of transformation.

FIGURE 25.
Seven-circuit Baltic
wheel or goddess

FIGURE 26.
Seven-circuit round
"concentric" classical

Roman Designs

These were seen from the period of the Roman and Byzantine Empires, 63 BCE through 1453 CE. They have anywhere from seven to twenty-two circuits with four quadrants and are square, circular, or sometimes polygonal.

> Fourteen-circuit square Roman (Figure 27)
> Nine-circuit round Roman (Figure 28)

Meditative Uses:

❖ Facing fears and transforming the self. ❖ Meditation of the spirit.
❖ Banishing negative thoughts and evil spirits.

FIGURE 27.

Fourteen-circuit square Roman

FIGURE 28.

Nine-circuit round Roman

Prayer Designs

These designs were seen from the Medieval to the Renaissance periods. They can be found in churches throughout Europe and in outdoor turf mazes. Like the Roman designs, these have anywhere from seven to twenty-two circuits, four quadrants, and can be square, circular, or polygonal.

Eleven-circuit Chartres (Figure 29)
Eleven-circuit Maltese (Figure 30)
Eleven-circuit Reims (Figure 31)

Meditative Uses:
❖ Pilgrimage to salvation. ❖ Meditation of the spirit. ❖ Redemption.
❖ Bringing oneself closer to the higher self.

FIGURE 29.

Eleven-circuit Chartres

FIGURE 30.

Eleven-circuit Maltese

FIGURE 31.

Eleven-circuit Reims

Man-in-the-Maze Design

From the Tohono O'odham and Pima Native American tribes. Unique unto itself, the opening symbol with a man at the top dates to the 13th century. This pattern is commonly seen woven into baskets.

Man in the maze (Figure 32)

Meditative Uses:

❖ Journey to transformation. ❖ Redemption of a troubled spirit.
❖ Bringing oneself closer to the sacred self.

FIGURE 32.
Man-in-the-maze

THE METHODICAL MAZE

Like the labyrinth, the maze also imitates nature. Sea coral (Figure 33) and the veined configuration of a common leaf (Figure 34) contain maze-like patterns. Although still winding like a labyrinth, the maze is more intricate and has multicursal or more than one pathway with many more choices of which direction to take.

The maze is thought to be a puzzle for the left side of the brain. With twists and turns, it exercises the logic of the mind into analyzing methodical solutions. While some say you lose your way in a maze, skill and process can be used to find your way out.

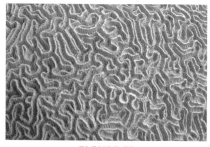

FIGURE 33.
Mazed sea coral

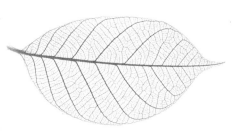

FIGURE 34.
The veins on a leaf

The biggest challenge of a maze is in moving through all the different roads. There are cul-de-sacs, dead ends, forks in the road, entrances and exits, and islands to name a few obstacles! Because of all these paths, the maze is designed to lead you to make meditative choices and solutions. These arise from situations created in the maze and lead to a final goal.

As previously mentioned, historical as well as modern mazes are seen throughout our culture today. Hedge maze gardens and turf mazes still exist throughout the world and are used as attractions for traveling visitors. Corn mazes are a favorite at harvest festivals taking place in autumn. Puzzle books with mazes especially for children are very common and used as learning tools in schools (Figure 35). Computer-generated games can be seen along the Internet highway with rising popularity (Figure 36).

FIGURE 35.
A children's book maze

FIGURE 36.
A computer-generated maze

TRADITIONAL MAZE TERMS

To understand mazes, you must first know the terminology of the pathways that can be contained in a single design. Identifying the different types of choices when traveling through a maze makes it easier to understand these complex patterns.

Maze Terms

Entrances/Starts and Exits: An opening into or out of the maze (Figure 37). Some mazes do not specify where the beginning or end is, and many have multiple openings.

Goal: This is an end point or exit, usually marked in the maze.

Branches: Pathways or passages in a maze.

Blind alley: This is a dead end where a turn-around is required.

Bottleneck: A pathway that connects one area to another. You must pass through a bottleneck to reach the end or goal.

Outside wall: Also known as the *boundary wall*, this is the outermost line containing the whole maze.

Cul-de-sac: Also known as a trap, these pathways loop around, backtracking to main paths.

Islands: Detached walls that are not connected to the outside wall of the maze.

Fork in the road: Where two pathways meet at a common junction.

Spiral: A path that winds into a dead end.

Vortex junction: An area where multiple pathways meet.

Room: Like the center of the labyrinth, this is an open area in the maze. It can be located at anyplace in the maze.

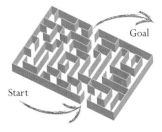

FIGURE 37.
Maze with start and goal

Types of Mazes

There are half a dozen primary types of mazes. Like the previously described labyrinths, each type has its own meditative uses.

Simply-Connected Maze

A simply-connected maze has no loop patterns. The paths do not reconnect with one another and every path leads to another path with one solution out. Keeping to the left-hand wall will guarantee a successful exit from this maze (Figure 38).

Meditative Uses:

❖ Effortless choice. ❖ Finding your way.
❖ Actions to take in obtaining a goal. ❖ Knowing the right direction.

FIGURE 38.
Simply-connected maze

Multiply-Connected Maze or Braid Maze

This type of maze contains many paths that loop back and forth and it may have dead ends (Figure 39). The braid maze is a multiply-connected maze with no dead ends.

Meditative Uses:

❖ Making powerful choices. ❖ Finding your way. ❖ Choosing a goal.
❖ Using your instincts. ❖ Knowing the right direction.

FIGURE 39.
Multiply-connected maze

Turf Mazes and Mizmazes

Turf mazes and mizmazes are actually labyrinths that have one path with no junctions or dead ends (Figure 40).

Meditative Uses:

❖ Finding your one true path. ❖ Meditation of the spirit.
❖ Allowing a journey. ❖ Facing fears.

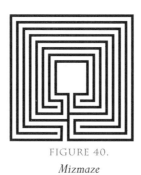

FIGURE 40.
Mizmaze

Weave Maze

In this type of maze, pathways weave under and over each other like bridges (Figure 41).

Meditative Uses:

❖ Making powerful choices. ❖ Finding your way. ❖ Choosing a goal.
❖ Crossing bridges. ❖ Knowing the right direction.

FIGURE 41.
Weave maze

Planar Maze

A maze not contained within a Euclidean (flat) space is called a planar maze (Figure 42). This can look like a maze on the outside of a cube or some type of spherical shape.

Meditative Uses:

❖ Making powerful choices. ❖ Finding your way easily within chaos.
❖ Choosing a goal. ❖ Using your instincts.
❖ Knowing the right direction. ❖ Expanding your capacity.

FIGURE 42.
Planar maze

CREATING A JOURNEY
ON THE PATH

You are now ready to make your meditative journey on the path. The following guide will help you through the different meditations while using the maze and labyrinth drawings. This is a creative process—whatever answers come to you are the right ones. The following steps have been designed to set you up to fully experience each meditation and its effectiveness.

MEDITATION

For our purposes, the use of meditation is to journey inward, bringing the mind, body, and spirit together for spiritual enlightenment. In a fast-paced world, the process of relaxing the body and quieting the chattering mind can be a profound, transformative practice. When we calm ourselves, the stresses of daily life seem to disappear. We feel more balanced, have more energy, and improve our health. Working through the designs will provide these experiences and more.

Different meditations in this book will be used for different purposes. For instance, there are some for healing, love, abundance, and harmony. The maze and labyrinth, by virtue of their constructions and sacred geometry, have different meditative purposes. You will find that choices and solutions will be attached to the mazes while the labyrinth meditations will mainly be concerned with birth, rebirth, and finding one's true path.

There are a few meditation techniques for you to follow. Make sure to relax your body with the meditative process guide. Don't forget to breathe. Breath is life, and the slower and deeper you breathe, the quieter and calmer you will become. Being still and forgetting about the outside world are the keys to success.

When working with the meditative process, the most important thing to remember is to open yourself as a channel for receiving. Giving up any preconceived notions or expectations is also recommended. Allow yourself to simply be guided by these ancient patterns. Letting the answers unfold will bring inspiration, messages, spiritual guidance, and transformation.

MEDITATIVE MAZE AND LABYRINTH GUIDE

The following steps are divided into three sections. Please read through each guided part as it will prepare you to use the drawings with meditative practice.

Part I. Getting Started

This is the first stage of your preparation.

Choose a drawing and suggested meditation. Make sure you are clear on the intention of the meditation and that you understand the questions.

Find a quiet, sacred space. This should be a place that is comfortable, peaceful, and where you will not be interrupted. If you are in a noisy or public place, try shutting out any distractions so you can focus on the task at hand.

Take out the drawing and pencils that you have chosen, and place them next to you for when you are ready to begin.

When you are situated, close your eyes and move on to the next part.

Part II. The Meditative Process

Follow this meditative relaxation process before beginning to color your selected drawing in Part III.

Close your eyes and take three deep breaths.

With every breath, begin to relax parts of your body, starting with your head. Release tension in the jaw, neck, and shoulders. Next, move down the arms to the hands, wrists, and fingers. Loosen the chest and release the belly and hips. Allow the thighs, knees, ankles, feet, and toes to relax. Let all negative energy run out the bottom of your feet. Take three more breaths, easing any remaining tension out of the body.

Once relaxed, notice if you have any discomfort or running thoughts. Just notice them. You do not want to try to fix, change, or analyze them. Being conscious of them will usually dissipate body pains and any thoughts.

Now your are ready to open your eyes and move on to Part III.

Part III. Meditative Drawing

Now begins the creative process. Follow these steps while coloring your maze or labyrinth.

Go to one of the following meditations. Read in your mind or aloud the intention and questions. Remember it is important not to answer or analyze the questions. Just allow the answers to unfold as you work through the designs.

Pick up your pencils and begin coloring. Make sure to start at the entrance or, if using a maze with multiple entrances, choose one. For the meditative purposes of these designs it is best to start at the beginning rather than coloring at random.

Color your design. This is where you get to use art as part of the meditative process. You may want to use multiple colors or various patterns (see "The Power of Color and Design," p. 33) to shade them in. It is recommended that you use whatever colors and patterns inspire you. You can't make mistakes and it does not have to be a perfect drawing—you're not aspiring to be Picasso. Your purpose is to use art to allow a flow and show your creative journey.

Try to color in the whole picture in one sitting to get the best result. If this is not possible, tell yourself that you will return at a later time to complete the drawing. When you return, go through Part II again and pick up where you left off. Some drawings may require multiple sessions.

When you are finished, review your work. Take note of any thoughts or experiences that you had while working through the drawing. This is a good time to write down any answers that may have been revealed to you regarding the questions in your mind.

Take a step back and view your drawing. You may even want to hang it up on the wall, bulletin board, or refrigerator. Notice what colors you used and how you colored it in. Sometimes your patterns may also answer the meditative questions. This is a good time to assess what you have learned from doing the meditation and coloring in the drawing.

THE POWER OF
COLOR AND DESIGN

The world was not designed in black and white, nor with straight lines, but rather with an array of spectacular colors and enchanting designs. Coming from nature itself, like a beautiful rainbow, colors and shapes have powerful effects on the mind, body, and spirit that we may not even realize. For instance, research has shown that being exposed to the color blue may produce a calming effect and reduce high blood pressure. Warm colors such as red, yellow, and orange stimulate activity such as eating and are generally used in restaurant décor. Advertisers often use circular shapes for selling products relating to a sense of comfort and connectedness while squares represent marketing goods for order and logic.

Knowing the meaning of colors and basic shapes is helpful for meditative practices. These can be used for therapeutic and healing purposes as well as gaining knowledge and understanding for your meditations.

Here are a few suggestions for coloring in your drawings:

- ❖ Try using a different color for each circuit or path.
- ❖ Experiment with different shapes, such as the triangle and square.
- ❖ Draw them on the path and then color them in.
- ❖ Make your designs two-toned, incorporating shapes like a checkerboard.

- Color in paths following the colors of the rainbow.
- The following color and shape charts are designed to give you added inspiration and powerful wisdom for coloring in your mazes and labyrinths.

THE POWER OF DESIGN

Designs have powerful meditative characteristics. They generate many different types of psychological responses, just like colors. We have seen shapes used on ancient artifacts as a way of communicating ideas. You may want to try using some of these within your drawings and then color them in. Here is a list of simple shapes and their meanings. You may want to make up and try some of your own.

CIRCLE: Connection, wholeness, love, comfort, feminine energy

SQUARE: Logic, security, order, linearity, masculine energy

TRIANGLE: Balance, strength, power, energization, knowledge

DIAMOND: Mystery, abundance, magic, solidness

COLOR POWER

Color energy from the rainbow has also been associated with the Indian philosophy of chakras in the body. Meditating on and working with chakras is an ancient art that has been used for centuries to heal the body. Each chakra has a color and represents a specific area along the core center of the body (Figure 43). The charts on the next page give meanings to both color energy qualities and the chakras.

Colors	Qualities
Red and pink	Energy, joy, vitality, courage
Orange	Daring, stimulation, happiness, confidence
Yellow	Imagination, intelligence, radiance, energization
Green	Balance, fertility, love, awe
Blue	Calmness, understanding, relaxation, expression
Purple	Clarity, protection, focus, intuition
White	Purity, peace, spirit, connectedness
Brown	Grounding, warmth, solidness

❖·❖·❖·❖·❖·❖·❖ THE CHAKRAS ❖·❖·❖·❖·❖·❖·❖

Color	Area	Inspiration
Red and pink	Root	I can have
Orange	Spleen	I can feel
Yellow	Belly	I can act
Green	Heart	I can love
Blue	Throat	I can be heard
Purple	Third eye	I can see the truth
White	Head	I can connect

FIGURE 43.

The chakras of the human body

MAZE AND LABYRINTH
MEDITATIONS

There are great gifts to receive from working with maze and labyrinth meditations. They are meant to enhance life by offering healing, spiritual growth, guidance, and transformational change.

This section offers four categories of meditations.

- ◈ Healing meditations
- ◈ Spiritual intuitive meditations
- ◈ Meditations for transformation and change
- ◈ Modern meditations

Each individual meditation notes whether it is intended for use with a labyrinth or maze. It will list which specific area the meditation is working on, such as love, forgiveness, or harmony. It will include an intention and a few questions you may want to ask yourself before, during, or after the meditation and coloring process.

Make sure to thoroughly read and understand each meditation before beginning. This will help you to get out of the mind and trust the meditative process.

Working with Labyrinths

Working with the labyrinths is a right-brained process in which you will use your creative mind, intuition, and trust. As you journey toward the center, see what you can overcome or release. When you arrive at the middle, it is best to confront any fears so you can move forward. Also, give yourself permission to accept any messages or gifts at this moment. Be open to receiving the process. As you exit the labyrinth, notice where you have arrived. This is the time to take note of any revelations or transformative thoughts.

Working with Mazes

As noted earlier, mazes are complex designs that use the analytical left brain. Because a maze may offer so many choices, there is no one way to work through them all. One thing for you to notice is how you react when you make a path choice and have to backtrack or go another way. This will give you access to processing your transformation with a particular maze meditation. Remember, maze meditations offer choices, decisions, solutions, and goals.

Tips
A few reminders before starting your meditative practice:

- There is no right or wrong way.
- Everything is as it should be.
- You don't have to be perfect or do this in a certain way.
- Give up any expectations or preconceived notions.
- Let go of analyzing, judging, or criticizing yourself and your work.
- Allow thoughts and messages to unfold.
- Enjoy yourself and the journey.
- Let your creative self be free to explore.
- Have fun!

Healing the Body

When we are not at ease, this usually manifests in the body as a "dis-ease." If you have pains or ailments, this meditation may give answers for healing.

Use: Labyrinths

Intention: To bring healing to the ailing body areas on a cellular level.

Questions:

What has caused this "dis-ease" or discomfort within my body?

How can I ease my pain?

What steps can I take to heal myself?

How can I be responsible for my well-being in the future?

Healing the Heart

This is a good meditation for broken hearts.

Use: Labyrinths

Intention: To complete painful experiences and allow the heart to feel all emotions so it can be healed and open to love again.

Questions:

What words or emotions do I need to express?

What can I be responsible for?

What do I need to release to be complete?

Forgiveness

This is quite possibly one of the hardest things to do when we feel wronged or betrayed. Meditating on forgiveness is actually the access to freedom in any given situation.

Use: Labyrinths

Intention: To be free of pain, betrayal, or hurt through the act of total forgiveness.

Questions:

What do I need to give up or let go of in order to forgive?

What do I need to say to have my peace?

Do I forgive totally and completely this situation or event?

Healing Relationships

This is different from healing the heart in that you may need to heal something that went wrong in a relationship. This can be some sort of a fight or disagreement with a friend, family member, or loved one. Use this meditation to give answers for healing the relationship.

Use: Labyrinths

Intention: To clean up any negative energy and restore or transform the relationship.

Questions:

What part did I play in this disagreement and where can I be responsible?
Can I agree to disagree and what can I release?
What is it that I like about being related to this person?
What is my apology and what promises do I make for the future?

Healing the Past

Sometimes we hold on to situations or events from the past in a negative way. This meditation helps to release and complete the old so we don't have to carry it with us anymore.

Use: Labyrinths

Intention: To allow past events to be bygones and to achieve a sense of completion.

Questions:

What words or emotions do I need to express or say around the situation?
Why am I holding on to the past?
What do I need to release to be complete?

Restoring Balance and Harmony

In a world that moves with a very fast pace, it is very easy to get out of balance. This healing meditation will restore harmony and balance in your daily life.

Use: Labyrinths

Intention: The scales of balancing life will become easy and harmony will be restored.

Questions:

What was I neglecting that caused disharmony?

Are there things I can eliminate so I can be in balance again?

Do I need to slow down?

What do I need to achieve harmony and balance?

SPIRITUAL INTUITIVE MEDITATIONS

Empowerment

This meditation offers guidance for restoring your own power. In this meditation it is important to be generous with yourself and imagine your power coming back into your body.

Use: Labyrinths, mazes

Intention: To reconnect with your power and restore confidence. To realize your power is never outside of yourself.

Questions:

Why do I feel powerless?

How can I be generous to myself and others?

When I am empowered what do I feel?

When I am empowered what do I think?

Creating Anew

Sometimes we need to create or birth new things in our lives and are not sure how to do it or where to begin. This usually applies to creating new situations, such as finding a new job or home. This meditation offers a starting point for ideas.

Use: Labyrinths

Intention: To create new things for yourself and your life with new energies and ideas.

Questions:

What old habits or things can I let go of?

What does my creative new life/job (or similar) look like?

What steps can I take to create it?

Receiving

For most of us, learning to receive can be a challenge, especially if we are not specific about what we want. Use this meditation to open up channels to receive those things you desire.

Use: Labyrinths, mazes

Intention: Being open and receptive to the gifts of receiving and aware of what you would like to receive.

Questions:

What would I like to receive?

Where am I stopped or blocked in receiving?

How will my receiving help others?

What steps can I take toward what I want?

Guidance

We look to friends and family for guidance, but rarely to ourselves. This meditation takes you inward to the stillness in your heart to find answers that can guide you in life.

Use: Labyrinths, mazes

Intention: To allow the messages of guidance to be received and trust that these are the right answers.

Questions:

Why am I seeking guidance?

Where am I confused and where do I need clarity?

What answers can help me in my situation?

What are the answers I am choosing to take on?

Making a Choice

Making a choice is one of the main concepts of the maze. If you find yourself in a situation that requires a choice, this meditation is ideal for facilitating a decision.

Use: Mazes

Intention: As you make your way through the twisted maze, your choices will become more clear and you will know what to do.

Questions:

What information do I have regarding each choice?

Is there anything else I need to know before making a decision?

What would the outcomes of each choice be?

What is my choice?

Finding a Solution

When we are faced with a problem, oftentimes fear and anxiety get in the way of finding a solution. Meditating with a maze and calming the mind will lead to clear resolutions.

Use: Mazes

Intention: The right solution to your problem will be revealed to you with grace and ease.

Questions:

What are the facts surrounding the problem?

What emotions of fear can I release?

What is the worst thing that could happen?

What solutions do I see?

What Are My Goals?

It is good to create a goal or vision for the future. This gives you something to live into. Mazes are great for working out the paths to your goals.

Use: Mazes

Intention: To be present in your goals and the steps to obtain them.

Questions:

What goal or goals would I like to create?

Are these goals grounded in reality?

What obstacles might I encounter in reaching my goals?

What steps do I need to take to reach my goals?

MODERN MEDITATIONS

These meditations correspond to the modern maze and labyrinth drawings. The beginning of each meditation tells you which picture to use. There are two sections—one for mazes and one for labyrinths. These meditations may also be used on the classic labyrinth and maze designs. It is suggested that you use the drawing recommended in the meditation for the best results.

LABYRINTH DESIGNS

Achieving Greatness

In this meditation, we look to the powerful bear totem to reveal our greatness. Achieving this quality takes much introspection as well as putting ourselves out in the world.

Use: Bear labyrinth

Intention: To see and experience the greatness of who you are.

Questions:

Where do I feel most powerful?

What challenges have I had to face in life?

What do I consider to be my greatest attributes?

How do I achieve greatness?

Opportunities

Opening up to opportunities is not always easy. In this meditation, you will explore being receptive and trusting the opportunities that come your way.

Use: Turtle labyrinth

Intention: To be open and receptive to new opportunities and to trust your intuition about acting on these opportunities.

Questions:

What preconceived notions can I let go of about opportunities?

Can I open myself to all opportunities?

Can I trust myself and my choices about such opportunities?

What opportunities would I like to create?

Being Heard

The dolphin represents sound, which translates into words for humans. Use this meditation to see where you need to speak up and be heard, or maybe there is something that you need to say. This also can mean expressing yourself in an area of your life.

Use: Dolphin labyrinth

Intention: To be totally heard and understood.

Questions:

Is there anywhere in my life where I have not expressed myself?

Is there anything I need to say, and, if so, to whom?

What is it I would say or need to express myself?

How can I let my voice be heard and understood?

Freedom

The meaning of freedom is to be able to live at will. Sometimes we become victims of our circumstances and feel as if we have no choices or freedoms in life. This meditation helps to see that we are not in chains and can create freedom in our lives.

Use: Eagle labyrinth

Intention: To see and experience places in your life where you can create freedom for yourself.

Questions:

Where do I not feel free?

If I were free in these areas, what would happen?
What steps can I take to achieve freedom?
What does it mean to me to be free?

Being Independent

Independence can be a scary proposition because we are left to our own decisions. The cat totem in this meditation helps you step into an independent nature of magic and mystery.

Use: Cat labyrinth

Intention: To bring about a sense of knowing and security in being independent, and to step into the mystery of the unknown with confidence.

Questions:

Who or what am I most dependent on?

Can I make my own choices and trust myself?

What constraints do I need to break free from so I can be independent?

What does being independent look like to me?

Strength

In life we may become weakened by a situation and not know where to begin to regain our stamina. In this meditation, we use the power of the horse totem to find our strength.

Use: Horse labyrinth

Intention: To face your weaknesses and regain power and strength.

Questions:

How and where did I become weak?

Do I forgive myself for my weaknesses?

What steps or things can I do to regain strength?

What will my newfound strength look like?

Transformation

Like the transmutation of the struggling caterpillar to the butterfly in flight we, too, experience transformations of struggle to freedom. This meditation offers help to see the end of strife and the light at the end of the tunnel.

Use: Butterfly labyrinth

Intention: To see any struggle in life as a transformative journey to freedom.

Questions:

What is my biggest struggle or challenge at the moment?

What can I do about it?

What lessons will I learn during this transformation?

What does the other side look like?

Family

Maybe we are having family problems or need to make decisions that will be best for our family. This meditation is intended to resolve issues and bring the family closer together.

Use: Tree labyrinth

Intention: To make choices that will be best for your family and to renew relationships within the family.

Questions:

Are there any problems with the family?

What does the family want?

What would be best for the family and our relationships?

How can these issues be resolved?

The Family Tree

It is always good to meditate on your family, who they are, and what they mean to you. Like the branches of a tree, they are an extension of you. Seeing their greatness builds a better life and stronger foundation for yourself.

Use: Tree labyrinth

Intention: To know your family and see the light that they are.

Questions:

Who is my family?

What do these people mean to me?

What amazing things have they taught me?

What is great about my family?

Unlimited Possibilities

It is always a good idea to meditate on unlimited possibilities in the universe. This is the first step in creating ideas that will manifest into the future.

Use: Solar system labyrinth

Intention: To think outside the box and travel into the universe to see your unlimited possibilities.

Questions:

What possibilities would I like to create?

Which ones do I think I can fulfill at this time?

What steps must I take to make these a reality?

Do I believe in my possibilities?

Seeing Clearly

Life can be cloudy at times and we need to wipe our eyes to be clear. This meditation can help us see clearly in any given situation.

Use: Eye labyrinth

Intention: With your vision and mind's eye you can see any situation clearly.

Questions:

What is being hidden from my view?

What am I in a haze about?

What must I face to be clear?

What is the truth so I can be clear?

Being of Service

There may be situations in which we want to help and may need assistance in how to be of service. The helping hand will give meditative advice about which direction to take.

Use: Hand labyrinth

Intention: The helping hand will guide you as to what service you can best offer.

Questions:

To whom or what would I like to be of service?

What services can I offer?

How will this service be of help?

How will I feel offering my services?

Calling in the One

When we find love, it is a mirror of ourselves. This meditation is designed to see the mirrored love you want to call into your heart

Use: Chakra labyrinth

Intention: To be specific about what type of love you would like to call into your life. Remember that this person is a mirror to you and be careful about how you create a reflection.

Questions:

Who will I be for the person I am to love?

What would I like from the one I am calling in?

What is the reflection I am creating?

What will our relationship look like?

I Possess the Right to . . .

For this meditation, go to the chakra colors earlier in this book and pick one of the body areas and colors that you want to work on. It is suggested that you use the color of the chakra in addition to other colors when drawing. Also, imagine a ball of the chosen color spinning in the corresponding area as you move through the labyrinth. You can also work with all the areas, coloring them in and asking the questions below.

Use: Chakra labyrinth

Intention: To heal and open up this chakra area with love and light and allow yourself to possess the right to _____.

Questions:

Why did I pick this area?

Are there any blocks in this area?

What healing do I want to bring to this area?

What has opened up in working with this chakra?

Protection

Nordic runes were a powerful source of divination used by the people of northern Europe especially for protection purposes. This meditation offers a seal of protection to keep out of harm's way.

Use: Nordic rune labyrinth

Intention: To love and provide light to surround you as a protective seal from any wrongdoing.

Questions:

Why do I feel I need protection?

What do I need to do to protect myself?

What protection surrounds me?

Maze Designs

Exploring Growth

It is always a good idea to look back at how far we have grown. Oftentimes we do not even realize how far we have come. This meditation is used to acknowledge our growth and see where we can grow in the future.

Use: Flower maze

Intention: To acknowledge the growth you've gone through in different areas of your life and to see new growth in your future.

Questions:

What changes have occurred over the last _____ month(s), year(s)?

What lessons did I learn and how did I grow?

What accomplishments can I acknowledge myself for?

What growth would I like to see in the future?

Wisdom

Trees are often associated with the wisdom of life. In this meditation, as you work through the tree, you will have the chance to reveal your own personal wisdom. Like a tree, you have lived many seasons and possess deep knowledge.

Use: Tree maze

Intention: The wisdom you carry inside yourself will be revealed to you.

Questions:

What have I learned in my life?

What knowledge do I carry with me?

What is the truth of my wisdom?

What special wisdom do I have to communicate to others?

Abundance

This meditation is recommended for calling in abundance as well as to see how much abundance we already have in our lives. Remember, this can mean a lot of different things. We can be abundant with money, love, health, material objects, and so on. When working with this maze, you want to be specific about what type of abundance you are envisioning.

Use: Sun maze

Intention: To see the areas of life where you are abundant, and to call abundance into specific areas of your life.

Questions:

Where do I have abundance in my life?

Where am I lacking abundance and what are my blocks?

In what areas would I like to create abundance?

What would I do with this newfound abundance?

Where Do I Star?

Many of us would never ask, let alone think about, the question, "Where do I star?" However, this is a good question to ponder in discovering where your talents lie. Usually, the place that we star is the most enjoyable place for us to be.

Use: Star maze

Intention: To discover where you shine in life as a star. Knowing that makes a difference for people.

Questions:

Where do I think I shine best in life?

Why do I think I shine in these places?

What feelings do I get when I am starring?
What effect does it have on others when I am shining?

Achieving Wealth

The rain maze has been chosen for this meditation because of the old adage, "When it rains, it pours." Certainly, in obtaining wealth, we would like a downpour. Use this meditation to see what obstacles may be in your way of wealth and what the easiest path is.

Use: Rain maze

Intention: To authentically bring wealth into your life with freedom and ease.

Questions:

What are my blocks or obstacles in achieving wealth?
Do I believe I deserve wealth in my life?
What are my feelings around having wealth?
What would I do with wealth if I achieved it?

Rebirth

The goddess is usually associated with rebirth. In this meditation, you will be focused on regenerating or rebirthing your life. When things become stagnant, we need to reboot and the goddess is the access to bringing in the new.

Use: Goddess maze

Intention: You are open and willing to step into a new era by allowing the rebirthing process to enter your life.

Questions:

What would I like to acknowledge from the past and let go of?
What are some new things I'd like to create in my life?
What gifts would I like to receive for my rebirth?
What will my rebirth look like?

Beauty

Our outer beauty and, especially, inner beauty are sometimes neglected or forgotten due to the hustle and bustle of our lives. Like the beautiful lotus flower that grows toward the sun out of the mud and muck of the pond, this meditation will bring to light the beauty within you.

Use: Lotus flower maze

Intention: Like a flower blossoming, you open up and see the light and magnificence of your beauty.

Questions:

Where does my beauty get neglected?

How can I care for myself more?

What is beautiful about me?

Compassion

Compassion can be seen as stepping into another's shoes and being mindful of what they are going through in life. Practicing compassion can bring us closer together with an experience of kindness and love.

Use: Meditation maze

Intention: To bring compassion to your heart and to see it radiating out into the world.

Questions:

Where am I most compassionate?

In what areas do I not show compassion?

What could I let go of to have a more compassionate heart?

What feelings do I experience when I am compassionate?

Truth

Using the symbol of the ankh, which represents life, this meditation focuses on the truths of our life. You can also use this meditation to find the "truth of the matter."

Use: Ankh maze

Intention: To see and experience the truth in your life or the truth of a situation.

Questions:

Do I see or think there are any lies or deceptions?

Are there any truths not being said?

What is the truth of my life?
What truth needs to come out?

Knowing the Self

Like the phases of the moon, we also have parts or phases of the self. For women it is termed "maiden, mother, and crone." For men it is the "knight, prince, and king." Use this meditation to experience the different parts of yourself.

Use: Triple moon sign maze

Intention: To experience the phases of the self and what they contribute to you knowing your true self.

Questions:

What is my maiden or knight like?

What is my mother or prince like?

What is my crone or king like?

How do these fit together in making me who I am?

Dreams

This meditation will help to let go of old dreams and discover new ones to live into.

Use: Dream maze

Intention: To achieve completion with old or failed dreams and move forward to realize new and exciting dreams.

Questions:

What dreams can I let go of?

For failed dreams, what experiences did I have or what did I learn?

What new dreams do I have?

Which dreams shall I start working on to make into a reality?

Love

Love can be incredibly complicated or very simple. This mediation has two different parts for exploring how you love yourself and another, and the type of love you would like to call into your life. You may choose to do both or just one.

Use: Love maze

Intention for the self: To be awakened and shown the love you have for yourself.

Intention for loving another: To see how much and what type of love you have to give to another.

Questions:

SELF

What do I love about myself?

What would I like to change about myself?

What can I accept about myself?

Can I love myself the way I am?

LOVING ANOTHER

How do I love?

Is there anything I can give up in loving another person?

Can I love unconditionally?

Gratitude

Being thankful is probably one of the highest virtues. Use this meditation in gratitude to bring yourself back to harmony and reality.

Use: Gratitude maze

Intention: To give thanks in your life for all the large and small things.

Questions:

What things can I be thankful for?

What little things can I find gratitude for?

To whom do I owe gratitude?

What can I thank myself for?

Joy

Joy is defined as the state of happiness or delight. Use this meditation as a boost of bliss, especially when you have had a bad day.

Use: Joy maze

Intention: To experience joy, happiness, and pleasure on a new level.

Questions:
Where is there joy in my life?
Where do I not have joy in my life?
When I am not experiencing joy, what can I let go of?
What makes me happy?

Peace

The tranquility of life often eludes us. To achieve peace, we take vacations or try to escape to somewhere quiet. This meditation will restore peace and harmony without needing to travel out of your home.

Use: Peace maze
Intention: To achieve a state of peaceful tranquility.
Questions:
Where am I not at peace?
What situations in my life are not peaceful?
What can I release to achieve peace in my life?
What does peace feel like?

Illustration Credits

Original maze and labyrinth inserts by April Burril

Figures 13, 14 (page 14), 16 (page 17), 22-32 (pages 19-22), 38-42 (pages 26-28) by April Burril

Chartres Labyrinth on Parchment on pages i-iii, v, viii, 1, 4, 16, 18 (Figure 21), 23, 29, 33, 36 ©Ecoasis/shutterstock.com

Page 2, Figure 1, ©Jari Bilén/shutterstock.com

Page 2, Figure 2, Cassandra Wass

Page 5, Figure 3, Public domain, scan by Simon Garbutt

Page 7, Figure 4, ©Janprchal/shutterstock.com

Page 8, Figure 5, ©AKV/shutterstock.com

Page 10, Figure 6, ©Cristina Ciochina/shutterstock.com

Page 10, Figure 7, ©Steve Holderfield/shutterstock.com

Page 11, Figure 8, ©Stephen Aaron Rees/shutterstock.com

Page 11, Figure 9, ©clearviewstock/shutterstock.com

Page 12, Figure 10, ©Chris Jenner/shutterstock.com

Page 13, Figure 11, ©kirych/shutterstock.com

Page 13, Figure 12, ©Christoff/shutterstock.com

Page 15, Figure 15, ©Zack Frank/shutterstock.com

Page 17, Figure 17, ©Keir Davis/shutterstock.com

Page 17, Figure 18, ©Larry Ye/shutterstock.com

Page 17, Figure 19, ©Kevin Renes/shutterstock.com

Page 17, Figure 20, Cecile Kaufman

Page 23, Figure 33, ©Edwin Verin/shutterstock.com

Page 23, Figure 34, ©Sapsiwai/shutterstock.com

Page 24, Figure 35, ©Telnova Anna/shutterstock.com

Page 24, Figure 36, ©3dsparrow/shutterstock.com

Page 25, Figure 37, ©Alfonso de Tomás/shutterstock.com

Page 35, Figure 43, ©kokitom/shutterstock.com